iSnooping on Your Kid

Parenting in an Internet World

R. Nicholas Black

New
Growth
Press

newgrowthpress.com

New Growth Press, Greensboro, NC 27401
newgrowthpress.com

Cover Design: Tandem Creative, Tom Temple, tandemcreative.net
Typesetting: Lisa Parnell, lparnell.com

ISBN-13: 978-1-938267-89-5
ISBN-13: 978-1-938267-32-1 (eBook)

Library of Congress Cataloging-in-Publication Data
Black, R. Nicholas, 1955–
   iSnooping on your kid : parenting in an Internet world /
R. Nicholas Black.
      p. cm.
   Includes bibliographical references and index.
   ISBN-13: 978-1-938267-89-5 (alk. paper)
   1. Computers—Religious aspects—Christianity. 2. Internet—
Religious aspects—Christianity. 3. Internet—Security measures.
4. Internet and children. 5. Parenting—Religious aspects—Christianity. 6. Child rearing—Religious aspects—Christianity. I. Title.
   BR115.C65B53   2012
   248.8'4502854678—dc23
                                                    2012026511

Printed in India

29 28 27 26 25 24 23 22   9 10 11 12 13

I t was during the second quarter of the Super Bowl that John's brother-in-law Tim logged onto the family computer to catch up on some work emails. As he cleared the history from the computer, he discovered some websites listed in the computer's recent history that troubled him. Tim alerted John's wife Cindy (his sister), and they viewed several extremely graphic pornographic websites that had been saved in the computer's history.

They assumed John was the viewer, but as they talked with him, they realized the assumption was wrong. The only other possibility was that Sam—John and Cindy's eleven-year-old son—was viewing pornography.

During the remainder of the game John paced in and out of the family-filled TV room, praying for words—words that would both confront and leave the door open for honesty. After their extended family left, Sam poked his head into the office and said goodnight. Before he hit the stairs, John asked, "Hey, have you been looking at anything you shouldn't be looking at on the computer?" Sam quickly replied, "Me? No, I haven't at all." John said, "OK, good." Sam started upstairs, but John gently stopped him and asked him to come back down to the office. "I'm going to ask you one more time, so think before you answer. Have you looked at anything you shouldn't have looked at on that?" John pointed to the computer. Sam paused, looked away from his father and then to the floor, and then said yes.

John reached out and embraced his son. During the next several hours his son confessed a daily habit of viewing pornography at certain "safe" hours, when the family schedule would allow him time on the computer alone. Other times were with friends at sleepovers, where they would use an iPod Touch, Internet-capable game console, or smartphone to surf pornography websites. Through his tears he described how badly he felt about himself and how powerless he felt while trying to stop.

How about Your Family?

Perhaps you can relate to John and Cindy, or perhaps something like this has already happened in your family. Maybe you haven't had to deal with this issue. But regardless of whether you have caught your child looking at porn, you need to be aware of the dangers of Internet porn and be prepared to protect and help your child so that he or she does not become trapped by it.

Parents are protective creatures. Healthy parents will guard and protect their children from nearly any danger. Kids are strapped into seat belts and constantly told not to run into the street. When they are older, they'll hear countless mini lectures on driving safely, staying away from drugs, and being home by 10:00 p.m. But some dangers keep lurking along the edges of life. You can't protect your children from every potential danger that's out there. Even for the best of parents, "protective fatigue" sets in, resulting in reduced vigilance for dangers that are less visible. When parents let their guard down—and we all do sometimes—it allows our children to walk through doors that can do great harm. Pornography is one of those doors.

Pornography can capture the mind and heart of a child or teen almost instantly. And it can set the stage for years of inner turmoil, along with depraved thinking, hiding, lying, and experiencing deeply broken sexuality. Porn produces a warped concept of sexuality and relationships, which years later can erupt with destructive force in dating, marriage, family, or vocation.

The fact is, almost every adult who struggles with sexually addictive behavior was introduced to porn at a young age. The sexual addictions sparked by pornography go on for years, hidden by the struggler, with parents totally unaware. One study showed that 90 percent of children ages eleven to sixteen had viewed pornography on the Internet.[1]

Today, through the Internet and cable TV, there is an abundance of entertainment options available. Social media, gaming, and video-sharing sites alone are transforming society at every level by granting access to people and visual media that most would never have encountered in years past. In addition, the ubiquity of portable devices that are Internet capable means you can see whatever you want, whenever and wherever you want. Having access to this media can be wonderful and enriching, but it can also be extremely dangerous.

It is this danger that parents are failing to notice and address in a way that will protect their children. To give children unrestricted access to the Internet is like unleashing them alone in a large urban city to find their way around. No loving parent would even think of doing such a thing! But many parents are not realistic about the sexual temptation their children are facing. Some refuse to admit their children could be lured by sex at all, while others are just overwhelmed and confused by the technology that's available. To make matters worse, parents rarely bring up the subject of sex, except to say, "Don't!" or "Wait until you're married." This combination leaves children and teens confused about their emerging sexuality and vulnerable to the constant bombardment of sexual material.

If you have discovered your child or teen has been looking at porn, the shock can be overwhelming. Some parents respond with anger and a hastily assembled response plan. They punish their child by temporarily confiscating his computer or mobile devices, and then try to restrict access by installing parental filters. Some brief discussions about sex might follow, but once the protective measures are in place, the crisis begins to fade into the past and the feeling that the family is safe again takes hold. Everything feels okay at this point. But it's not.

The discovery that your child or teen has looked at porn cannot be quickly addressed as a single incident and left behind. As devastating as it is to discover that your child has looked at porn, it is important to see this situation as a gospel opportunity. Now is the time to engage the heart of your child and point them to the only One who can wash them clean and set them free.

Psalm 119:67 says, "Before I was afflicted I went astray, but now I keep your word." Affliction—whether it comes by unexpected suffering or consequences from our own or someone else's sin—is an opportunity to renew our relationship with God and learn to practically apply the gospel to our everyday lives.

Redemptive Responses to Discovering Your Child Has Viewed Pornography

1. Control your anger.

It's okay to be angry when you discover your child has been looking at porn. But make sure to direct your anger at the sin and not at your child. James 1:19–20 says we should be "slow to anger; for the anger of man does not produce the righteousness of God." The anger you direct toward your child or teen will have the likely result of making them incapable of hearing your concern for their safety and character; they will only remember your rage.

Instead, direct your anger against the brokenness of this world and the evil one who tries to corrupt and destroy everyone. Keep in mind that your child lives in a world where he or she constantly hears messages that twist and pervert God's good gift of sex. When you remember these truths, you will be in a better position to constructively help your child because you will understand the difficulty of trying to live a life of sexual integrity in a world that has gone sexually insane. Allow the compassion that flows from understanding their struggle to transform your anger and direct it at the real culprits. Allow God to comfort your grieving heart as you work with your child to understand what kept calling them back to porn.

2. Go after their heart, not their behavior.

Whether your child has been caught using porn or has confessed it on his own, work to stay calm and engage his heart. Ask him questions, not just about his porn usage, but about what drove him to look at these pictures.

- How did it start?
- How did you feel about doing this?
- How long have you been looking at porn?
- What do you think about what you have been seeing?
- What circumstances tend to trigger a desire to look at porn?

Ask whether he can understand some of the messages that porn communicates and teaches (power, control, false intimacy, escape from stress, degradation of women and men, and so on). Children and teens need to know how to discern the motives of their hearts. They need to learn that it is from the inner recesses of the heart that behavior and all of life flow (Proverbs 4:23).

This is an opportunity to offer the deep comfort of the gospel in the midst of deep brokenness. Don't only attempt to shut down access to porn as if that were the end of the matter. Your children need to learn that we all sin because our hearts desire it, not simply because we have access to it. If your response to this crisis is to redirect bad behavior through parental control alone, you will not be helping your child learn discernment or understand the rebellion of his heart.

Our children need to be taught that their behavior doesn't come out of nowhere, but is fueled by what they want or desire. Ever since Adam and Eve decided that what they *really* wanted was to be in charge of their own lives and not listen to God (that's what sin fundamentally is), our desires (even for good things) have become corrupted. Your child might want any number of things when they use pornography: pleasure, excitement, escape from pain, comfort, power, intimacy, control, confidence, relationship, and so on. Your questions can help them sort out what is really going on inside them when they turn to pornography. At bottom, their pornography use adds up to putting something at the center of their lives instead of God. The apostle Paul in Romans 1:23–24 said that sinful living is the result of fallen hearts that "exchanged the glory of the immortal God for images made to look like mortal man and birds and animals and reptiles" (NIV). In other words, sexual sin is about active idolatry, where we "exchange the truth of God for a lie" (v. 25) and live for something—anything—to satisfy our desperate hearts instead of turning to God. Do you see how this event is not just about behavior? It's much deeper than that.

By engaging them with questions and biblical teaching you will be communicating your love for them, a love that is strong enough to address their hearts and shepherd them through the difficulties of life. Chances are good that your child is struggling with shame and guilt over her behavior, and a loving, grace-filled approach will give her a flesh-and-blood taste of the love and grace that Christ gives to sinners. As you do this, direct your child to Christ to ask for his forgiveness and his grace and strength to handle her sexuality in a God-honoring way.

3. Maintain an ongoing discussion about sex.

Your child's porn usage will fling open the door for discussing sexuality whether you like it or not. But even if your child hasn't been using pornography, now is the time to teach your child about God's design for sex. Teach them that it is good and created for our good, and that its expression is only properly displayed within the safe and healthy boundaries set by God. Acknowledge the difficulty everyone has, especially adolescents, to live God-honoring lives of sexual integrity in a world of perpetual sensuality. However, also give them hope that as they cling to Christ and his word, this is not an impossible task.[2]

A crucial way to help your children see this hope is to keep the conversation going. They need your shepherding to grow up well, and that includes being shepherded through the turbulent years of their sexual development. There is no such thing as having a one-time talk about sex and then sending them on their way. Pornography will deceive your child's heart and distort sex in extremely harmful ways. Now you must guide them toward God's wonderful design for sex so they can delight in the truth and uproot the lie they have believed.

Do not underestimate their need for you to talk about sex in healthy ways! If sex is treated like a bad word, your child will be left with conflicting messages. Sex will appear as something that adults do but never talk about. This will make it seem shameful, like a dark secret to be hidden. If you don't keep talking about sex at opportune moments, your child will be left alone to interpret all the images of the porn they have seen. If those images are not brought into the light of God's truth, they will continue to pull and tug on the mind and heart. This will only increase the desire to view more porn and further distort the way they think and feel about sex.[3]

But in your discussion about sex, they need to learn why pornography is dangerous to their emotional, physical and spiritual development. It's not just about looking at images of naked bodies. Here you will need to explain to them the "messages" porn teaches, and how those messages radically distort sexuality and relationships, and lead to disastrous consequences.

• Porn disconnects sex from relationships. It turns real people into objects to be used. It teaches that the sexual act is what matters, not the person you need to build a loving relationship with. It's a false view of what sex was created for.

• Porn disconnects sex from love and respect. Much of porn is full of aggression and violence, and continual looking at porn can shape one's behavior, especially toward women. It teaches self-centeredness; it's all about me and what I want.

• Porn disconnects sex and relationships from human dignity. Porn's ugliest "underbelly" is its ability to push what is perverse to previously unheard of levels. And the more one keeps looking at porn, the tendency is overwhelming to look at edgier and more extreme images, thereby "normalizing" perversions.

• Porn is addictive. God's gift of sexuality to us is incredibly powerful, and for that reason children and teens need guidance on understanding it and managing it for the right and best reasons. And as mentioned earlier, addictive behavior produces hiding, deceit, lying, covering-up, guilt, shame and extreme selfishness, which will eventually destroy relationships, careers and one's walk with God.

• Porn contributes to global abuse and injustice. Looking at porn is not a harmless, private activity. Viewing it, engaging in it, contributes to the entire "system" of broken sexuality throughout the world, and a great many of those involved in the production of pornography come from abused and broken backgrounds and situations.

4. Examine your own heart.

If you are going to own your parental role of shepherding your child's sexuality, then you must be living within God's design for it. You will not be able to help your child if you are engaging in porn or other out-of-bounds sexuality. Here is another way the grace of God can surprise as he pursues you. He will use suffering and struggle in your children to show you what you need to learn about your relationship with him. Now the opportunity afforded by this crisis is not just about your child, it includes you. As mentioned earlier, suffering, whether it comes unexpectedly or as a consequence of someone else's sin, is an opportunity to renew our relationship with God as we learn to lean on his shepherding care and guidance (Psalm 119:67).

If your own sexual behavior is sinful, now is the time to draw near to Christ and ask for his forgiveness and grace to change (1 John 1:9–10). You cannot lead someone where you are not first willing to go yourself. Accept Jesus' forgiveness and grow in his grace, and as you grow in this area of struggle you will find yourself being an honest and authentic help to your child.

Should you admit and confess your own struggle to your child? It depends. If he or she is young, it's probably not wise. But if your child is an older teen, it may be a great opportunity to appropriately share some of your struggles and the way you are experiencing grace and obedience in Christ. You can do this without going into graphic detail. Your child needs only to know the general outline of your struggle, but you can be very specific and detailed about how you are going to God every day for forgiveness and help. Your children can grow tremendously in the faith when they see their parents as imperfect people who must cling to Christ in order to grow in faithfulness and obedience.

5. Block the door.

Not allowing access to harmful Internet and media is extremely important. You might find it challenging to do this and also respect your child's privacy. While this has always been a source of tension, today our politically correct culture preaches a false gospel of tolerance that twists freedom into license. Consequently, many parents are timid, hesitant, or overwhelmed with techno-savvy teens clamoring for freedom. But rampant parental naiveté or an unwillingness to do the hard work of oversight is contributing to a massive corruption of our youth. Denial or unwillingness to do the parental work needed here will leave your child or teen wide open to being ripped apart by the evil one. "Be sober-minded; be watchful. Your adversary the devil prowls around like a roaring lion, seeking someone to devour" (1 Peter 5:8). Lions are opportunistic predators, and the prey they go after the most are the young. Satan is like that too.

So is it appropriate to snoop on your teen's use of the Internet and other high-tech means of entertainment and communication? *Yes! You absolutely must!* But how you go about doing it is critical.

Ephesians 4:15 instructs us to be "speaking the truth in love," and Galatians 5:6 says that "the only thing that counts is faith expressing itself through love" (NIV). One of a parent's most important jobs is to help their children build character, and one aspect of character is sexual integrity. This means having a sexuality that is owned and used for their good and God's glory. Children do not build character on their own, and developing sexual integrity doesn't just happen. Part of keeping the discussion about sex going is to know and see what your child is doing.

But snoop respectfully. Snoop in the open and in a way that communicates that you have their best interest at heart. Let your children know that you will oversee their online behavior and do not feel or act guilty about doing it. Love confronts and restrains when necessary. This gives your child the biblical boundaries he or she needs and can help to protect them from further involvement in Internet porn or inappropriate online relationships.

Practical Advice on How to Snoop Respectfully

1. Get help! Technology is growing and changing quickly, and few parents have the time to stay on top of all the changes. If you are not technologically up to speed, get help from friends who are. They can keep you in the know on the latest techno dangers and help you set up protective systems. If you do not have a friend like this, find one quick! If you can't find someone to help you, then hire someone to assist you. It's that serious!

2. Make a plan with your family for safe Internet use. Sit down with everyone in your family and discuss the good and bad things about the Internet and technology. Speak directly about the dangers of unrestricted media access. Lay out a protective plan for everyone in the family to participate in (including you, the parents!). No one is safe in this always-on online world. If you set up a plan that only involves checking up on your kids (and leaving you as parents outside those protective parameters), then they will, over time, resent your protective oversight and may go "underground" in their online usage. Children think in terms of fairness, and although that doesn't always make sense, it should here. Just as parents would not think of serving their children broccoli while they ate steak, they will help their children agree to and accept a family plan by participating themselves.

3. *Expand your protection plan beyond the computer.* In today's world, your protection plan cannot just be the family computer! Parents and kids now own multiple Internet-connected devices (desktops, laptops, smartphones, cell phones, iPads, iPod Touches, game consoles, Internet-connected TVs, and so on). A good protection plan must encompass all these devices, or the loopholes will be big enough to drive a truck through! Make sure your plan is comprehensive. Also, think twice about giving your child or teen a smartphone. They are powerful computers that can access any site on the Internet using a cell phone carrier's wireless system. Do you really want your children to have a device that can tempt them anywhere? It's safer to have a simple cell phone that cannot access the web. If you

do allow them to have a smartphone, see point number five below.

4. *Find a program that covers all of your home, Internet-connected devices.* A program like FamilyShield from Open DNS is a great place to start (www.opendns .com/familyshield). Installing this program will restrict websites on every Internet-connected device in your house that uses your home's Wi-Fi router. Pay special attention to make sure no one uses proxy sites. Proxy sites are websites that allow someone to access inappropriate websites without leaving a trace of history behind. OpenDNS blocks these proxy sites. Protecting Internet access at your home at the source—your router—is the best place to start. As an added safeguard, it may be necessary to also use a parental filter offered by your Internet provider or purchased from another company.

5. *Install safe browsing and tracking software.* Mobile devices can access the Internet outside the home using data plans or Wi-Fi hotspots, so Internet usage outside the home is wide open to abuse. Therefore, install safe browsing programs and tracking/accountability software programs such as Covenant Eyes, CyberPatrol, NetNanny, or others on every computer and Internet-connected device. Consider also using an accountability tracking program that can send you an e-mail or text message when one of your kids accesses or tries to access a restricted website. Accountability software can be especially good for teens, as they need more freedom to make wise choices as they grow

older, and this software can provide not just oversight, but a forum for discussion between you and them as you see what they are looking at.

6. *Restrict time usage on your computers.* Doing so will keep your kids from being online obsessively, and it recognizes that sometimes filters fail. Know the times your kids could be most vulnerable (after school when no one is home or late at night), and set your computers to shut off during those hours.

7. *Monitor Facebook and other social media sites.* Talk with your kids about using social media sites like Facebook. You need to monitor Facebook like you would monitor your child's friends at school and in the neighborhood. Pay close attention to the privacy settings in Facebook and check up on them regularly. Facebook frequently changes privacy rules without notifying users. Setting the privacy settings to "Friends Only" is a good place to start, but you'll need to be vigilant about what this allows. Insist that your child give you his Facebook password. In fact, insist that your child give you all of his online passwords. This should be part of the "family plan of protection" mentioned in point number two.

8. *Check those apps and instant messaging services.* Apps are what is driving online usage today, particularly on mobile phones and devices, and it is here where our kids are facing very real danger. There are a number of apps that are used as ongoing chat rooms where kids can face terrible ridicule and bullying. Some apps are sexual "hook-up"

apps, and even teens are using them for sexual encounters with total strangers. Bottom line: you have to know what apps are on their devices and know which ones are safe and which are dangerous. Because so many new apps are becoming available constantly, you need to go into a search engine and ask: "What are the dangers to kids using (type name of app)." Then read the links. If the app looks questionable, talk with your kids about the dangers and why they shouldn't use it. Then remove it. For young children, go into their mobile device settings and disable the downloading of all apps. Then, when they want a certain app to use, go research it with them to decide whether it is safe or appropriate. Then, you download it and reset the settings.

9. Be cautious of fantasy or role-playing sites. These sites allow teens to experiment in creating other (alter) identities. These sites can help some kids who are socially awkward to learn social skills and even develop good relationships through appropriate online games. But for other kids, such sites can encourage false intimacy and a preference for belonging to a virtual community over real relationships. Know your child and know the websites he visits. If you see your child preferring to spend his time online instead of socializing with real people, step in and talk to him about it! Engage his heart to find out what is motivating him in this direction, and take steps to help him bring about a healthy balance. Create "computer free" time periods that you can fill with real living relationships.

10. Keep testing your protection. Once you have installed all your protective systems, regularly "test the locks" to see if everything is working properly. Nothing is foolproof, so check regularly. Setting up these safeguards is going to cost money, but do not hesitate to spend it. Your kids are worth it! One simple, no-cost method of protection that should also be used is to require that all Internet-connected devices be used in the open in the presence of other family members.

11. Check your child's Internet site usage. Use your tracking/accountability software and check the browser's history. Keep in mind that browsers today have "private browsing windows." Make it clear that use of these is akin to lying, which means they shouldn't be used. Unfortunately, it is easy to erase one's Internet history, either on a computer or on a mobile device, so you need to make this a character issue with your children. Impress on them the dangers of engaging in lying, deception, and cover-up as a lifestyle. Don't forget to randomly check all their Internet-connected devices (cell phone pictures, text messages, smartphones, and the like).

12. Pay attention to search engines. Search engines can be highways to porn. Search engines also display images, and those images can be very explicit and pornographic. Set strict safe-search parameters (use the strictest parental settings on all search engines and password-protect them if that option is available) or consider only using safe search engines (you can find them on the web). Most search engines will have family safety tools to help you here. Use them! But keep in mind that search engines "leak" all the time. Sites that display porn or sexually explicit images (like some blogs) multiply almost by the minute, and it is impossible to block everything.

13. Be wise about overnight sleepovers. Overnight sleepovers can be a prime time for porn exposure or other sexual experimentation. Assume other families (even church families) do not take these matters as seriously as you do. Talk to your friend's parents about your concerns regarding Internet usage before your children go over. That may be awkward (and your kids may not like it!), but many parents have not even given a thought about the dangers. Remember, you are not imposing your standards on them, just raising the issues and asking them to honor your values, for the safety of all the children involved. Make sure your kids have a clear plan of action, including calling home for a ride, if they find themselves in any compromising situations.

14. Monitor video communication. Video communication is growing rapidly. Make sure all such programs (Skype, Facetime, and so on) have the strictest and most private profile settings, and that they are never used alone late at night. It goes without saying that chat rooms should be off-limits or severely restricted and closely monitored.

As you do your best to monitor your child's Internet use, keep in mind that the most important thing is to keep the conversation going. The two worst mistakes are to do nothing at all ("My kids wouldn't do these things! We're Christians!") or be so fearful that you lock everything down like a Federal prison. The former will leave your children defenseless, and the latter will not help your kids grow in wisdom and learn to make wise and healthy choices about what they look at or spend time on. We are all using more technology, and that trend is only going to get stronger. At the same time that you are checking on them, keep talking with them about why you are doing this and how much you love them and want them to build good character. Don't make this into "big brother" is watching you. Instead, give them "permission" to use your checking as a peer-pressure defeater. Point out to them that because you are checking on them, they can say to their friends, "I can't do *that* because I *know* my parents will find out." This can provide the hedge of protection your kids actually crave.

A loving and growing relationship with your kids will protect their dignity as individuals, while allowing them to see your protective care. You want your children to feel that it is safe to come to you when they struggle. Their trust in your love will make it easier for them to give honest answers when you ask about their Internet usage. Make certain that all these protective measures are embedded in the bigger picture of God's story of redemption. It is not enough to spend your time trying to keep your kids from Internet porn. You must also teach them about the beauty and wonder of sexuality as designed by God.

Don't Let Up or Give Up

Remember, although you need to impose oversight, this is not just a behavior issue to be fixed with controls. Though it is appropriate to be angry and saddened that your child has seen and engaged in porn, at least you are aware of it and can take to shepherd him or her away from it. Many kids never get caught, and they end up wrestling with deeply entrenched sexual addictions as adults. It is always God's mercy when our sin is exposed!

One last point: anticipate failure. Your kids are sinners like you are. James points out that, "we all stumble in many ways" (James 3:2). Because our hearts are inherently sin-stained, we remain vulnerable to untold numbers of temptations and failures. You and your children will never be sinless this side of heaven. Remember, keep in mind that they are facing a battle for sexual integrity that can feel overwhelming. They need your protection and your grace-filled shepherding. When they stumble and fall, talk with them about what was happening in their hearts, and extend to them the same forgiveness and grace that Jesus Christ has given you. First John 1:9 is a passage of hope for going forward in life after failure and sin: "If we confess our sins, he is faithful and just to forgive us our sins and to cleanse us from all unrighteousness."

By not condemning them for their failure, you will keep the lines of communication open and increase the chances that the next time they struggle, they will turn to you. Let them see your help as coming from one who also needs help from God to live life as he calls us to live it. Demonstrate to them how important it is to ask for and receive the help of others. Let these stumbles be transformed into new opportunities to exult in the good news of forgiveness in Christ, for both your child and yourself.

Endnotes

1. In 2001, a study by social psychologists at the London School of Economics showed that 9 out of 10 children (ages 11 to 16) had viewed pornography on the Internet (Sara Gaines, "Why Sex Still Leads the Net," *The Guardian*, 28 February 2002. Web. 4 Dec. 2009. http://www.guardian.co.uk/technology/2002/feb/28/onlinesupplement.newmedia)

2. For a longer discussion of God's design for sexual intimacy, see my minibook, *What's Wrong with a Little Porn When You're Single* (Greensboro, NC: New Growth Press, 2012).

3. For clear, kid-friendly advice, see William P. Smith's minibook, *How to Talk to Your Kid about Sex* (Greensboro, NC: New Growth Press, 2011).